SPIRIT & TRUTH

52 Devotions for Law Enforcement

ADAM DAVIS

Printed in the United States of America.

ISBN-13: 978-1507819463

ISBN-10: 1507819463

To the men and women who faithfully hold and support The Thin Blue Line.

CONTENTS

ACKNOWLEDGMENTS

There are so many people who must be acknowledged who made this possible. From proofreaders, beta-readers, and those who have supported my mission on social media, thank you.

To my wife and children for their undying love and support while I commit my gifts to the Father, I could not do this without you.

As a citizen, I value law enforcement. In fact, I believe that you're a minister of the Lord. That's exactly what the Apostle Paul said, "The police aren't there just to be admired in their uniforms. God also has an interest in keeping order, and he uses them to do it." (Romans 13:4 Message Version) God uses police officers in the protocol of authority so that all things are in good working order and protecting the living and commerce within our communities. Your positional authority is under God to flow benefits to those whom you serve, the citizenry of your community. Remember, you are an agent for God, as such, you are not going it alone. You are in His service.

This devotional is designed to be a weekly encouragement to you. As you read it, meditate on its promises, be strengthened in your resolve to serve honorably toward not just man, but to God, as He is your commander.

Neil Kennedy, Author & Founder

FivestarMan.com,

Be Strong & Be a Man! 1 Kings 2:2

JANUARY

Justice is a joy to the godly,
but it terrifies evildoers.

— PROVERBS 21:15
NLT

PEACEMAKERS

WEEK 1

Many times, in law enforcement as well as any other professions, there are days when so many issues are dumped on you at once, everything seems so overwhelming. In these times, I can tell you without a doubt that God keeps His promises. It is not God's will for you to be overworked and stressed to the max! Jesus said before He ascended into heaven that the Father was sending a Peace giver known as the Holy Spirit.

The peace of the Holy Spirit is a peace that surpasses all understanding. Seek His peace today, and not the peace that any thing, person, or thought can give you as a fellow brother. Seek His power, His will, and His way. He is more than you need, and His peace will come abundantly to you!

Yes, my soul, find rest in God;
my hope comes from him.

— PSALM 62:5

Weekly Thought:

When you are discouraged, remember why you began your career in law enforcement. God's promises are true, even though His responses are not on our clock.

Practical Application:

Find a way this week to recognize God's peace in your life. Take five minutes and thank Him in advance for His protection, His peace, and His forgiveness. Don't ask for anything in this prayer; just thank Him.

Prayer

Heavenly Father, thank you for giving me peace in the middle of turmoil and chaos. -Amen

NEW MERCY

WEEK 2

I will be the first to admit that I find it difficult to show mercy when someone harms me or my family, especially my wife and children. How do we think God feels about us when we repeatedly fail? His love never fails, and there's nothing we can do to change His love for us. What reassurance and comfort in knowing there's nothing we can do to change God's heart for us!

But having the love available to us and receiving it are two different things. He's waiting on us to reach out and accept His love and mercy. You have full access to the power of God!His Word says His mercies are new every morning. Seek help from the Lord when someone seeks to destroy you! Show mercy, walk humbly, and be generous with forgiveness.

> *Has God forgotten to be merciful?*
> *Has he in anger withheld his compassion?*
>
> — PSALM 77:9

Weekly Thought:

Are you freely showing mercy and grace to others, as often as you would need it? Encourage each other this week as you seek wisdom and discernment in uniform.

Practical Application:

When someone wrongs you this week, I challenge you to show mercy toward them.

Prayer

Heavenly Father, thank you for the gift of mercy and love. Help me to reach out and accept your gifts and power for my life this week.

POWER TO LOVE

WEEK 3

Do you recall how you felt during your first adrenaline-pumping encounter as a law enforcement officer? I remember how exactly how I felt. I loved it! It was exhilarating! But not every kind of love is that way. I understand and know there is a time we must be warriors, but there is also a time to deliver love. How do we deliver truth? With firmness and kindness and love.

Consider this type of love like the seasoning on your food. If your food is past its expiration date, bitter, nasty, or without flavor, it will be rejected. Cover your actions of serving today in love. And don't forget your family when you get home. If you are married and/or have kids, take ten before you get home to clear your mind. They don't deserve to pay the price for the stuff you dealt with at work.

Do everything in love.

— 1 CORINTHIANS 16:14

Weekly Thought:

Don't allow the things of this world to affect your love and passion for Christ. He can revive your love for Him, His Word, your family, and your profession.

Practical Application:

Ask God to revive your passion and desire for a relationship with Jesus. Pray for God to help you understand His Word, the *Holy Bible,* as you read it daily.

Prayer

Heavenly Father, thank you for the life-changing, life-empowering, future-altering love you have for me.

ABUNDANT GRACE

WEEK 4

So, what do we do with grace? Is it like the worn out duty belt we wear on every tour of duty? We use it when we need it, but, *only* when we need it, right? Nope. In fact, I have been guilty of grace abuse more so than I care to admit. Yes, we have free will, and yes, God forgives.

However, I suggest that when your best friend hurts you, you forgive him without delay. Does that mean you want him to continue hurting you? No, of course it doesn't. Perfect love overcomes and His grace is sufficient. Today, if you are feeling overwhelmed with the things of life, remember, you have been given the power to overcome.

Walk in grace today and know God is with you.

What shall we say, then? Shall we go on sinning so that grace may increase?

— ROMANS 6:1

Weekly Thought:

How do you define grace? Have you even ever considered it? Take some time this week to dig into what God says grace really is and then practice it.

Practical Application:

Find an area of your life, an area you want to change. This is between you and God, and when you identify it, ask God to help you make the changes you need to. Then, take some practical steps toward working within the faith you demonstrated in your prayer.

Prayer

Heavenly Father, thank you for the abundant grace readily available for me in life. Open my eyes and change my heart to see the power of Your grace.

FIRM HOPE

WEEK 5

"I sure hope we aren't busy tonight." The sentence slipped from my lips, no harm intended from this rookie. Little did I know I'd just spoken an unspeakable word to my fellow officers. Everyone at the table stopped eating on the spot and exclaimed, "Next call is yours!" What had I done?

What have you hoped for? Are you weary in battle? Have you experienced too much hurt, negativity, and pain? Jesus doesn't only give us hope, He is our hope. He delivers on every promise, just sometimes not in our timing. Don't lose hope today, brothers and sisters! God's got this battle; accept His hope as you move forward with confidence.

For in this hope we were saved. But hope that is seen is no hope at all. Who hopes for what they already have?

— ROMANS 8:24

Weekly Thought:

We have heard many public figures tell us how they could bring us hope. Their intentions were likely solid, but there is no hope without Christ as the centerpiece of the message.

Practical Application:

Do you believe we have hope? The Bible gives us clear instruction on what needs to happen for our land to be healed. Repent, pray, and seek the ways of God above our own.

Prayer

Heavenly Father, I know my only hope is in You. I willingly turn from the sin I have in my life and ask you to show me the way you have for my life.

FEBRUARY

God blesses those who work for peace,
for they will be called the children
of God.

— MATTHEW 5:9 NLT

RUN WITH ENDURANCE

WEEK 6

How many physical agility tests did you have to take before you got hired on at your respective agency? What about after you got hired? Running builds endurance; endurance builds character; and according to Romans 5:4, this is what gives us hope. Begin your journey of faith in Christ if you haven't already.

I encourage you to begin small, taking baby steps to build your endurance. Take time to write down or record the things God is doing in your life, to get started. Building your physical endurance is necessary, but so is building your spiritual endurance. This life is a marathon, not a sprint, but He's given you the power to endure and persevere.

Not only so, but we also glory in our sufferings, because we know that suffering produces perseverance; perseverance, character; and character, hope.

— ROMANS 5:4

Weekly Thought:

We all know someone who has fallen by the wayside when it comes to physical conditioning. The same applies to our spiritual conditioning. We must encourage others in their faith journey, even when they stumble and fall.

Practical Application:

If one among you stumbles, lift him up. Be an encouragement to someone this week.

Prayer

Heavenly Father, thank you for the persevering power of your Spirit in my life. Have your way in my life.

KNOW YOUR WORTH

WEEK 7

We have all been in situations where our reputations were on the line. A good reputation and credibility are priceless in the law enforcement profession, as they are in many professions.

You can possess all the talent, skills, knowledge, and ability in the world, but as a law enforcement officer without credibility and respect, you will not go far. Stand tall in adversity; earn your worth. It isn't always determined in dollars, skills, but in your willingness to live obediently before God in all you do. How will your worth be determined? Follow through with the commands God has given you and watch Him open doors for success.

A good name is more desirable than
great riches;
to be esteemed is better than silver
or gold.

— PROVERBS 22:1

Weekly Thought:

Stocks rise and stocks fall. What determines stock value? Generally speaking, it is the performance of a company or product, maybe even a service. Essentially, the dollar amount given for the stock is the opinion of people. How will people think of you if you are not trustworthy and honorable? Your stock will be weak.

Practical Application:

Ask God to show you how you can improve your relationships at your agency. Ask Him to show you how much you are worth to Him. Prepare to be amazed!

Prayer

Heavenly Father, help me to see my worth through my identity in You.

FORGIVEN

WEEK 8

We have all, at some point in our lives, made some pretty bad mistakes. We have all messed up, sometimes pretty badly. Let's take a moment and forget our mistakes and instead, look at the power of forgiveness. There is much more to forgiveness than the words "I forgive you," or in some cases, "I forgive me." I am talking about the removal of guilt. Only the power of God's forgiveness can remove the guilt of our sins and I encourage you to embrace that.

Move forward and leave the junk behind you. Yes, in your heart, you have to forgive those who hurt you, regardless, and you have to forgive yourself for your mistakes. Let them go!

You forgave the iniquity of your
people
and covered all their sins.

— PSALM 85:2

Weekly Thought:

Isn't it amazing how God not only forgives us, but He removes our guilt? How awesome is that? If you still have guilt in your heart about past mistakes, take some time to ask God to help you deal with that.

Practical Application:

Do not keep records of wrongdoing, especially with your spouse. In the next devotional for law enforcement marriages, I will get into this a little bit more. If you want to experience God's removal of guilt, forget about someone else's hurt and wrongdoings against you.

Prayer

Heavenly Father, thank you for the reminder that I have been forgiven by You, and You take all my shame and guilt.

FOREVER FAITHFUL

WEEK 9

I have been horribly guilty of falling to the wayside; there is no denying it. After the first couple of years in law enforcement I found myself questioning my faith. My heart was very cold, very sick, and very hurt. It was a long process, and is still an ongoing process, but God is doing a work in my life. He alone has the power to completely heal our lives and our minds through His Word, creating pure thoughts in us, and making us faithful once again. Our faithfulness belongs first to God and then our families. But our brothers and sisters in blue, they are on the list too. We are all family, and through faithfulness and loyalty to each other, the brotherhood and bond can be restored and strengthened where needed.

Create in me a pure heart, O God,
and renew a steadfast spirit
within me.

— PSALM 51:10

Weekly Thought:

Were you once an active believer in Jesus? Stop for a moment to remember what that looked like for you and think about why you don't see that in your life now. Your former faith can be restored and I can offer you suggestions that have helped me.

Practical Application:

God renews our minds through the reading of His Word. What does that mean? Read the Bible! You can download The Bible app (from Life Church) for Android and Apple iPhone products for free. Spend some time daily in His Word. That is the first and biggest step. The Lord renews our minds and He makes us faithful once again.

Prayer

Heavenly Father, thank you for the power to remain faithful in all I do.

MARCH

Everyone must submit to governing authorities. For all authority comes from God, and those in positions of authority have been placed there by God.

— ROMANS 13:1 NLT

STRONG IN DUTY

WEEK 10

There are always those who are stronger than us. It never fails that someone will always be stronger, faster, in better shape...you name it, and there is always someone *better*. But nothing compares to the supernatural strength bestowed on us from God. I am not only talking about spiritual strength, but physical strength.

There are many recordings in the Bible of God enabling those who were physically weaker than their opponents. Trust in God, put your faith into action, and with the two combined, you will be prepared for the fights in life.

I love you, Lord, my strength.

— PSALM 18:1

Weekly Thought:

God gave Samson great physical strength. In the same way, He gave young David great power as a shepherd and as a king. You are no different. God will give you the power, the strength, the words, and the tools you need for your job.

Practical Application:

In order to be spiritually strong you have to be connected to the power source. Ask God this week to help you become stronger spiritually. If you spend an hour in the weight room, spend an hour in the prayer room as well.

Prayer

Heavenly Father, thank you for the strength I have in You.

PERSEVERANCE = VICTORY

WEEK 11

I have already mentioned endurance in an earlier devotion; however, this use of the word *endure* is a bit different. It's a call to *persevere.* Enduring difficult times is something none of us truly look forward to. However, these are inevitable and even necessary times in life. We all know this to be a fact, but what do we do with them? I once heard a pastor talk about driving in stormy weather. He recounted how he would just keep going," regardless of the storm. In life, we have to do the same. I don't need to tell you that, but what I *can* tell you is something I've learned: If we keep moving, regardless of how bad our circumstances are, no matter how small the steps we take, we *will* come out of the storm.

Because you know that the testing of your faith produces perseverance.

— JAMES 1:3

Weekly Thought:

Do you have feelings and thoughts of inadequacy when it comes to your faith? If you have issues understanding the Bible, or God in general, do not worry! God is much bigger than we can imagine—in so many ways! We were not designed to figure God out; we were designed to be His children and to put our faith in Him.

Practical Application:

Much like we focus on our physical stamina in our profession, we must also work to persevere in faith. When you face trials and troubles in life, do not quit. Do not walk away. It often seems easier to give up, but ask God this week to give you strength to endure the tough times.

Prayer

Heavenly Father, thank you for total victory in life in every area as I submit to Your ways.

PREVAILING JUSTICE

WEEK 12

Why did you take the oath of a police officer? What about wearing a badge, a gun belt, driving a police car, and law enforcement appealed to you in the first place? Most respond with, "I wanted to help people" or "I wanted to serve my community." Others are more honest: "I wanted to drive fast." Regardless of your reasons, deep down you likely wanted to bring order to chaos, preserve peace, and serve in justice. Wouldn't it be awfully boring if peace and justice ruled "every mountain and every hill"? While we don't get to deliver justice every single day, facing us is the real consequences for some. Let the wisdom of God guide you in preserving peace and justice.

The mountains shall bring peace to the people, and the little hills, by righteousness.

– PSALM 72:3

Weekly Thought:

As law enforcement officers, we have a great deal of responsibility on our shoulders every day, even when we're off duty. There are those who look to destroy our lives and even take our lives. Do not allow the negativity of this world affect your calling and passion.

Practical Application:

Ask God to give you wisdom this week. His Word says He'll give it if we just ask! God will give you wisdom relating to every area of your life and law enforcement; now just ask Him for it.

Prayer

Heavenly Father, thank you for reminding me that vengeance comes from You alone and that, in the end, justice will prevail.

LIFE'S REALITY

WEEK 13

For a long time I thought fairness and justice were the same thing. Then I realized if they were, the Old Testament would not have made as many references to "fairness and justice" together. Fairness is not showing favoritism or impartiality. What is fair, then? Life certainly isn't; we all know this to be true. Being fair is simple: treat others the way you want to be treated. Being fair means not doing something to anyone else you wouldn't want done to you. It also means treating individuals equally under the same circumstances.

Be fair and just in all your duties and seek to honor God with your work.

And he shall judge the world in righteousness, he shall minister judgment to the people in uprightness.

— PSALM 9:8

Weekly Thought:

This is going to be a little bit elementary, but it fits and is necessary. "Do unto others what you would have them do unto you." Just apply the Golden Rule. Although this may not apply to law enforcement as a profession, still, be fair.

Practical Application:

Ask God this week to show you how you treat others unfairly, if you do. Make a conscious effort to make the changes you need to in order to express fairness to everyone.

Prayer

Heavenly Father, I know You are working all things together for my good as I seek Your purpose for my life.

FIRM FOOTING

WEEK 14

Holding back a wall of protestors is something law enforcement officers across America have dealt with many times. Perhaps it's an angry crowd at a crime scene where only two officers are on hand. Regardless of the situation, God gives us strength to stand tall, be strong, and stand firm. Where you are weak, He gives strength. When we are weak, He is strong.

It is important to remember that God doesn't change, and the same God who caused the enemies to fall in the Old Testament and throughout the Bible can move the enemies in your life. Stand firm and be courageous.

They are brought down and fallen:
but we are risen, and stand
upright.

— PSALM 20:8

Weekly Thought:

Maybe you wonder where God is at when bad things happen. God does not desire or permit harm on His people. His promise is that He is with us through it all.

Practical Application:

Standing firm is not always easy. Each time we receive a domestic dispute call, a disorderly person call, or any call for that matter, we are required to be vigilant and alert. Use the gifts God has given you. Stand firm in your faith this week. Ask God to give you strength and courage to do this continually, even in the most challenging situations.

Prayer

Heavenly Father, thank you for strength to stand.

APRIL

But in that coming day
no weapon turned against you will
succeed.
You will silence every voice
raised up to accuse you.
These benefits are enjoyed by the
servants of the Lord;
their vindication will come
from me.
I, the Lord, have spoken!

— ISAIAH 54:17 NLT

COURAGEOUS WARRIOR

WEEK 15

Psalm 138:3 says "When I asked for your help, You answered my prayer and gave me courage." It really is that simple. Just because we put on a vest, gun belt, and badge, doesn't mean we can't have access to God for our needs. He cares about police officers too! Use the gifts God has given you. Stand firm in God's help, guidance, and wisdom. He will listen and respond.

What are you asking God for in your life right now? Don't be discouraged if you haven't seen an answer yet. He hears your cry and will give you the boldness and courage to pursue, if you will be willing to obey His direction and leading.

When I called, you answered me;
you greatly emboldened me.

— PSALM 138:3

Weekly Thought:

Not everyone who is courageous has the best abilities at the firing range. Not everyone who responds one way under normal circumstances will respond the same way under stressful circumstances. Build each other up in courage.

Practical Application:

Ask God to help you this week as it relates to being courageous. For most of us who wear the blue uniform, courage is second nature; otherwise we would not be in this profession. However, there may be some around you who lack courage. Before you take action against them, ask God how you can help them develop courage, before it is needed.

Prayer

Heavenly Father, thank you for discernment, wisdom, common sense, and courage for battle.

USING FEAR FOR YOUR GOOD

WEEK 16

The Bible says that the battle is not flesh and blood, but of principalities and powers in the air. While this is just a paraphrase, we know that with terror, ambushes, and random attacks comes fear. It would be easy to allow fear to creep into our minds and hearts as law enforcement officers, but don't let it! Fear is crippling.

Remember the story of David and Goliath? Yes, the same story many people have heard since they were children, *that* David and Goliath. God used a scrawny kid to defeat a giant. He can certainly use us to defeat the most intimidating enemies in this life.

And many of the brethren in the Lord, waxing confident by my bonds, are much more bold to speak the word without fear.

— PHILIPPIANS 1:14

Weekly Thought:

Fear can be a powerful tool for us to use, if it is harnessed. Do not live from a place of fear, but use it for good.

Practical Application:

Ask God to give you power over fear. In the New Testament, God's Word says He hasn't given us a *spirit* of fear, but of power, love, and a sound mind. Ask God to give you this power, love, and a sound mind this week so you can move forward with authority, clarity, and in love.

Prayer

Heavenly Father, thank you for teaching me through Your Spirit how to be victorious in this life on every level.

AN EMBOLDENED SERVANT

WEEK 17

While I'd like to say I have always been bold, the truth is I haven't always been bold as I should've. But I love to talk to people and when I'm needed to perform a duty on the job I do it. You probably do as well. But what about sharing our faith?

Do you find it difficult to be bold in sharing your faith? Sometimes I do. I don't suggest we shove our beliefs down the throats of others or engage in debates with them.

But be bold this week; not only in duty, deeds, and strategy, but also in your walk of faith. God will honor your faithfulness.

Wait on the Lord: be of good courage,
and he shall strengthen thine
heart: wait, I say, on the Lord.

— PSALM 27:14

Weekly Thought:

Law enforcement changes us; let's admit it. Think about the way you would sit in restaurants before taking your oath and how you do now. Be bold enough this week to approach God in prayer. Tell Him where you are weak and ask for His strength.

Practical Application:

The Bible says to "boldly approach the throne." God has created you uniquely. Don't you think God knows how law enforcement officers are wired? Ask God this week to give you a boldness for Him, for your duties, for your marriage, and for your family.

Prayer

Heavenly Father, thank you for supernatural boldness, and wisdom to use it for Your glory.

SUPREME JUDGE

WEEK 18

We only have control over enforcing the law. We prepare cases, write detailed and accurate reports, and complete thorough investigations. But sometimes the courts do not find the defendants guilty. But think about it: Have we ever been guilty of wrongdoing? Yes, we have. Do we have the right to determine the level of severity when it comes to sin? No, we don't.

While the laws we enforce have different degrees of severity, sin is sin. We are all guilty of sinning. But His forgiveness is amazing! His Love is everlasting and His mercies are new every morning. You may be guilty, but God is telling you to go free! Live freely today through God's forgiveness.

Strive to live a pure life following Jesus.

> *It is not good to accept the person of the wicked, to overthrow the righteous in judgment.*
>
> — PROVERBS 18:5

Weekly Thought:

We've all heard that we all sin; we all mess up. Do not give in to this excuse. Make a choice today to allow God to clean up your messy life, your messy mind, and give you strength to walk the walk (and not just talk the talk).

Practical Application:

Live open-handed. Let go of those things that have caused you secret shame and guilt. When we surrender our lives to God, He does amazing things!

Prayer

Heavenly Father, thank you for wiping my slate clean and giving me power to walk in total victory.

DECLARATION OF INNOCENCE

WEEK 19

Much like the suspect we've arrested on the streets for multiple crimes, do we sit now looking to God insisting we are innocent of sin? Let us not be foolish! Each of us has sinned, and tremendously at that! Each of us has fallen from the grace of God and has been in very dark places. Yes—we are guilty, with no need to proclaim our innocence; there's a price to pay for sin, whether that price is paid here in this life or in eternity.

The good news is Jesus already paid the price for you and me, and all we have to do is accept His gift and honor His word in our lives. When we do this, we align ourselves with His will and His power is made available to us.

If God places no trust in his
holy ones,
if even the heavens are not pure in
his eyes, how much less mortals,
who are vile and corrupt,
who drink up evil like water!

—JOB 15:15-16

Weekly Thought:

Call upon the name of Jesus; He will come to you and He will rescue you.

Practical Application:

Just try it. You've had enough interest to read this far in the devotional, so you must want to learn more about a life of surrender to Jesus. Believe. Repent. Live.

Prayer

Heavenly Father, thank you for power to address the evil in this world, and the goodness to overcome it!

MAY

This is my command—be strong and courageous! Do not be afraid or discouraged. For the Lord your God is with you wherever you go.

— JOSHUA 1:9 NLT

CONVICTED

WEEK 20

How do you feel about that nudge in your gut? The nudge that says, "Don't do it!" We all have a tendency for sin, having been born with a sinful nature. Yet God convicts us. Some people refer to His conviction as your conscious. God is the one who convicts us eternally for our sins.

Here on earth, being convicted can mean a couple of things; it can be that voice in your gut, or it can be the result of a court proceeding. None of those matter as much as being convicted by God's power.

Listen to Him.

One witness is not enough to convict anyone accused of any crime or offense they may have committed. A matter must be established by the testimony of two or three witnesses.

— DEUTERONOMY 19:15

Weekly Thought:

It may be easy for some to resist temptation, but for others it may not be so easy. It may be too easy for some to ignore that voice of warning. Don't ignore that voice speaking within you. It's the Holy Spirit warning you of sin and danger.

Practical Application:

Ask God this week to make you more sensitive to His conviction. He will steer you, guide you, and straighten your crooked paths.

Prayer

Heavenly Father, Thank you for the access to your mercy, grace, and forgiveness.

WE ARE FREE

WEEK 21

S*he was found not guilty. He was acquitted.* These are some common phrases in law enforcement. However, enforcing the law is different than trying the case. The enemy of our souls stands to prosecute us for our sins. God the Father sent His Son Jesus as our defense.

Jesus is our defense and when He gave His life for us He took care of all eternal punishment we were justified to receive. He stands ready, pleading our case, as long as we believe in Him and put our trust in Him, we will be acquitted in the end. Walk away clean! No probation, no fines, and one day, your eternal reward will come to you.

You have not given me into the
hands of the enemy but have set
my feet in a spacious place.

— PSALM 31:8

Weekly Thought:

Jesus had the power and ability to call on God the Father and be removed from the cross at the crucifixion. In fact, He didn't have to endure the beatings or the whippings. He gave His life for you, for me, and for every other life that has been lived.

Practical Application:

Ask God to set you free from whatever binds you this week. There is an awesome freedom found in a relationship with Jesus, following His Word and living by His principles.

Prayer

Heavenly Father, Thank you for the freedom that I can only experience through a relationship with You.

A POWERFUL KING

WEEK 22

We have an advocate in Christ Jesus. He has given each of us power over the enemy, our adversary. We have certain powers bestowed on us from our jurisdictions as law enforcement officers, but the power God gives is greater. Too often we become focused on the challenges in this life and not on the power He has given us to be victorious.

His power sustains us, propels us to victory, and brings us through dark places. Stop cutting yourself short in the trials of life and look for the blessing in the battle.

Trust His power, and experience God in a way like you have never seen. Watch and see.

I have given you authority to trample on snakes and scorpions and to overcome all the power of the enemy; nothing will harm you.

— LUKE 10:19

Weekly Thought:

If God has given us the power, as Luke 10:19 says, to trample snakes and scorpions and defeat the power of Satan, then why do we cut ourselves short? Let's not sale ourselves short when we have access to supernatural strength and power through Jesus.

Practical Application:

Ask God to show you His true power this week. Ask Him to show you where He has made you strong, so you can show your gratitude for His strength.

Prayer

Heavenly Father, thank you for the authority over the evil in this world.

GUARD YOUR WEAPON

WEEK 23

Recent events across our country have left officers ambushed after riots, protests, and mayhem following grand jury decisions in Ferguson, Missouri, and Long Island, New York. But evil and chaos have dominated this world long before we ever strapped on a gun belt or pinned on our badges. We aren't battling against mankind, their actions are only representative of the darkness and evil they've bought into.

Begin today to live in a way that will leave a godly legacy for your family, and let your life be a constant reminder of the power and strength God gives. More importantly, begin speaking this Scripture over your life before your tour of duty.

> *No weapon forged against you will*
> *prevail,*
> *and you will refute every tongue*
> *that accuses you.*
> *This is the heritage of the servants of*
> *the Lord,*
> *and this is their*
> *vindication from me,"*
> *declares the Lord.*
>
> — ISAIAH 54:17

Weekly Thought:

I have a lot of questions, some of which I think I shouldn't have to have. For example, why would a believer in Christ, who wears the blue uniform, shield, and gun belt, be ambushed and murdered? The enemy is hovering over, looking for someone to devour. Be vigilant. Be strong, wise, and faithful.

Practical Application:

Ask God to provide you with supernatural

protection as you serve. I have seen His power work, as you hopefully have as well.

Prayer

Heavenly Father, thank you for shielding me from the attacks of the enemy, and giving me discernment to see it coming.

JUNE

Praise the Lord, who is my rock.
He trains my hands for war
and gives my fingers skill for battle.
He is my loving ally and my fortress,
my tower of safety, my rescuer.
He is my shield, and I take refuge
in him.
He makes the nations submit
to me.

— PSALM 144:1-2 NLT

FIT FOR DUTY

WEEK 24

Being a law enforcement professional requires great strength, stamina, and endurance. Not only physical strength, but mental and emotional strength are also required of us. Are we fit for duty? Look at Luke 17:10 for an example.

Maybe the thought of being spiritually fit for duty never crossed your mind, or maybe you haven't given it much consideration recently. What opportunities are you missing out on by not accessing the rewards He has for those who place Him as Lord and King of their lives?

I am going to challenge you this week: Take an

internal inventory of your life. If today was your last, would you be counted worthy?

> *So you also, when you have done everything you were told to do, should say, 'We are unworthy servants; we have only done our duty.'*
>
> — LUKE 17:10

Weekly Thought:

Do a weekly regular check to ensure you are fit for duty.

Practical Application:

Ask God to give you the motivation, encouragement, and support system to ensure you remain fit.

Prayer

Heavenly Father, thank you for prompting me by Your Spirit to focus on spiritual fitness more than my physical fitness.

EMPTY THREATS

WEEK 25

David was a mess! In the book of Psalms we read a lot of David's writing, from the time he was a shepherd throughout his time as a king. As a king David messed up a lot. If God would listen to David, an adulterer and a murderer, He will certainly listen to you. But, when we place our way above the priority of worshiping the King, we become misaligned and miss out on the plan God has for us. If we want Him to hear our prayers, we have to align ourselves with what His word says we are to do.

He hears you when you pray. Be a man or woman after God's heart. The way to His heart, begins in His word, and through prayer.

Hear me, my God, as I voice my complaint;
protect my life from the threat of the enemy.

— PSALM 64:1

Weekly Thought:

Most of the news on television these days leads to discouragement and depression. Eventually, we get to the point where fear begins to dominate our lives. Do not let the threats of various enemies cause you to fear and tremble. Take your concerns to God.

Practical Application:

If you are burdened down with care, take it to God in prayer. If David, a man of much power, was wise enough to take his issues to God in prayer, don't you think you should too? Establish a lifeline with God. He will breathe fresh life into you!

Prayer

Heavenly Father, thank you for peace amidst empty threats and invalid complaints.

VIOLENT ENEMIES

WEEK 26

The risk is ever present. It's there when we exit our patrol cars, exit the station, or even sit down to eat a meal. The risks and threats of a violent enemy attack hover over us daily. How do we respond to this? Do you believe there is a greater, higher power offered from God's protection?

Here's the promise of God, that He will lift you up above those who seek to destroy you, that He will deliver you and empower you.

Call out to God through prayer, seek His will and direction. He will deliver you. He will provide you with wisdom, discernment, and protection if you incline your ear to Him.

Who saves me from my enemies.
You exalted me above my foes;
from a violent man you rescued me.

— PSALM 18:48

Weekly Thought:

The family of blue bloods across America is facing an exponential growth in threats. They come from every angle. We cannot prepare for every scenario, especially an ambush. But what we can do is depend on God.

Practical Application:

Ask God to give you discernment, to speak to you, to provide you with supernatural protection. He will do so. I promise. Just believe.

Prayer

Heavenly Father, thank you for saving me from my enemies and giving me victory over those who seek to harm me.

ARE YOU HURTING?

WEEK 27

Have you been physically injured? Emotionally injured? How is your spirit? God offers healing through the reading of His Word and the gathering of His believers. He will provide a path to reconciliation if you are hurting. Don't lose hope. There is a way to peace and healing, no matter what your situation is. Whether it's relationships, work, or finances, God is in control. He will give you the solution you need. As my friend Neil Kennedy said in his book *God's Currency*, God doesn't rain down pennies and dollars from heaven..." Indeed, God does not, but He will give you a creative and capable mind with which to move forward.

to the One who gives victory to kings,
who delivers his servant David.
From the deadly sword

— PSALM 144:10

Weekly Thought:

There are so many hurting people in our world, many of whom are law enforcement officers. If you are having a tough time in life, I encourage you to seek someone to talk to, whether it be a counselor, a pastor, or a friend. Talk to someone and put your faith into action.

Practical Application:

Ask God this week to give you someone to confide in. As law enforcement officers, we are generally reluctant to open up about our own concerns and therefore we harbor hurt, pain, and thoughts. Don't hold on to those things! Let them go.

Prayer

Heavenly Father, thank you for peace and healing in times of pain and attacks.

BLOCK OUT THE PAIN

WEEK 28

Have you ever messed up real bad? How do you respond to the pain of failure? As law enforcement officers, we are aware that one mistake on our job can make for a really bad day for us, our families, and our department.

Don't let the pain of fear become a disabling factor in your life. Don't let the fear of failure imprison you. If the day comes and setbacks are in front of you, know that God's strength and Presence are with you and you are more than a victor.

My heart is sore pained within me:

and the terrors of death are fallen upon me.

— PSALM 55:4

Weekly Thought:

The pain associated with guilt can be overwhelming. The pain associated with fear can be incapacitating. We are not designed to live in fear. Do not allow fear to be the motivating factor behind your decision making in life. Learn to overcome and conquer fear.

Practical Application:

Ask God this week to give you peace. If you are dealing with issues relating to anxiety, God can give you His unspeakable peace.

Prayer

Heavenly Father, thank you for tenacity to work through the pain of setback and failure. Strengthen my heart!

JULY

There is no greater love than to lay down one's life for one's friends.

— JOHN 15:13 NLT

DIVISION & DEFEAT

WEEK 29

If one of us were to prepare for duty, respond to calls, and perform the duties of a law enforcement officer all on our own, we would be overwhelmed. Not only overwhelmed, but we would be in a position of failure. This is an issue many departments face, for various reasons, in our country today. But if we work together as one, we position ourselves and our team for greater success.

I appeal to you, brothers and
sisters, in the name of our Lord
Jesus Christ, that all of you agree
with one another in what you say
and that there be no divisions
among you, but that you be

perfectly united in mind and thought.

— 1 CORINTHIANS 1:10

Weekly Thought:

We are called to be peacemakers. Naturally, there will be those who oppose our efforts of peace. We must be persistent in our efforts to overcome the pain of fear and the fear of failure.

Practical Application:

The Bible says we have not because we ask not. Ask God this week to give you the peace you need. He will not only forgive you, but He will also remove the guilt of sin.

Prayer

Heavenly Father, thank you giving me the wisdom to navigate divisive situations and relationships.

POWER IN UNITY

WEEK 30

There is tremendous power in unity. How do we achieve unity among our surroundings? What about our agencies? There will always be people who stir the pot, so to speak, but we must learn how to communicate our words in love.

God will give us the wisdom to handle confrontation. With unification in mind we can confront with gentleness without causing division.

Make every effort to keep the unity of
the Spirit through the bond
of peace.

— EPHESIANS 4:3

Weekly Thought:

Be a vessel of peace, therefore being the bond of unity. Use your words wisely and let your actions reflect such.

Practical Application:

How do you deal with the person who always causes division and turmoil? They may not be within your agency, but they do exist. Ask God to give you wisdom. You may not be in a position of dealing directly with this person or people, but He will give you wisdom and discernment on how to appropriately deal with the situation.

Prayer

Heavenly Father, thank you for the power of unity in my life and I operate and live in unity.

IN DUE SEASON

WEEK 31

Proverbs 4 discusses the seeking of wisdom. Wisdom brings great value to our lives; I have found this to be true in my own experience. In time, wisdom will promote you in life. Are you up for a promotion within your department?

If you have the experience, seek to find within you the relevant knowledge and wisdom and apply it appropriately.

Cherish her, and she will exalt you;
embrace her, and she will
honor you.

— PROVERBS 4:8

Weekly Thought:

What is wisdom? Are you wise in your decision making? Do your research this week as to the definition of wisdom and look at the decisions you are making in life. If you seek and ask for wisdom, you will not regret it.

Practical Application:

Ask God for wisdom. Above all other things in life, seek wisdom. If King Solomon, arguably the wealthiest person to ever live, tells us wisdom is the most valuable gift we can ask for, we should search for it more than anything else in this world.

Prayer

Heavenly Father, thank you for the unction to seek wisdom above other things. Above it all, Lord, grant me Your wisdom!

EXPERIENCING GROWTH

WEEK 32

If we want to experience growth in our lives and in our professions, we must step outside of our comfort zones. Have you ever been frustrated when you see wicked men and women flourish and grow? When I tell you their growth is temporary, I mean it. As believers in Christ, our hope is in an eternal reward. We need to establish relationships with those in our lives who are wiser and those who want to grow. If you want to grow, step out of your comfort zone.

The righteous will flourish like a
palm tree,
they will grow like a cedar of
Lebanon;

— PSALM 92:12

Weekly Thought:

Jesus had twelve disciples. He poured His life into them. Find a place where you can be discipled in the Word of God. This may be a small group, a church group, or just meeting with like-minded believers in your agency.

Practical Application:

Are you complacent? Maybe you are too comfortable in the place you are at in life and work. Ask God to pry you out of your comfort zone this week. Believe me, He will. It is time to flourish.

Prayer

Heavenly Father, thank you for growth! Help me to endure the pains of growth, and to follow your plan and not my own.

AUGUST

The wicked run away when no one is
chasing them,
but the godly are as bold as lions.

— PROVERBS 28:1 NLT

SERVANT LEADERS

WEEK 33

Do you remember training with handcuffs when you began your career in law enforcement? Maybe you've even been cuffed for some very real reasons. There is a freedom when those chains are removed! When the chains of sin are taken from us, we experience a freedom like never before. As law enforcement officers we are servant leaders.

This means we live a life of servanthood; we are truly expected to "serve and protect." Look at the life of Jesus. He was not a wimp, a weakling, or a pushover. Some of the greatest leaders in our lifetime and before us were servant leaders. This does not mean we are weak.

Truly I am your servant, Lord;
I serve you just as my mother did;
you have freed me from my chains.

— PSALM 116:16

Weekly Thought:

As believers in Jesus, we have been set free! He has taken us from a destination of eternal death, to eternal life, and life abundant here on earth!

Practical Application:

There are some great books on servant leadership and there are some great examples in the Bible of servant leadership. Ask God to show you some examples of true servant leadership.

Prayer

Heavenly Father, thank you for the call to serve your people as a law enforcement officer.

HEAVENLY AGENTS

WEEK 34

As law enforcement officers we are the first line of defense between peace and absolute horror. God the Father sent His only son to intervene on our behalf. Jesus came for you, me, and everyone else. He came to bridge the gap sin caused between us and eternal life. We serve a very important role in our communities, bridging the gap between danger and peace for our citizens. Don't take the responsibility of being the gap between chaos and order lightly.

For there is one God and one
mediator between God and
mankind, the man Christ Jesus,

— 1 TIMOTHY 2:5

Weekly Thought:

Jesus could have called on a heavenly host of angels to remove Him from the cross, but He didn't. He followed His Father's plan for peace. Our responsibility as law enforcement officers is great, but the reward for being the true peacemakers in our world is beyond our thinking.

Practical Application:

Ask God to use you this week as His agent, His mediator. He will use your words and your actions to bring peace and bridge the gap in difficult situations.

Prayer

Heavenly Father, thank you for the gift of your Son, Jesus. I know the source of my peace is You. Amen

DESERVING OF PUNISHMENT

WEEK 35

When a criminal is caught, convicted, and sentenced, his punishment is earned—agreed? What about us, though? Do we reject the love of God, the price Jesus paid for us, and the eternal reward He has prepared for us? I recall a statement one of my first pastors told me, "Don't do anything stupid!" If we do something stupid, or, deal "professionally" with someone else who had done something stupid, let us deal with prudence, wisdom, and firmness.

The prudent see danger and take
refuge,
but the simple keep going and pay
the penalty.

— PROVERBS 22:3

Weekly Thought:

Let us be thankful for the good things in life. It is important to take time to be thankful and count our blessings. Be thankful for the good things and be thankful for the tough times as well. We can derive great wisdom from our mistakes.

Practical Application:

Be prudent in your actions. Do not overlook the word of God. Ask God to show you the secrets of His Word.

Prayer

Heavenly Father, Thank you for mercy when I deserve the worst punishment of all. Thank you that Your mercies are new every day. Amen.

GOD'S WILL

WEEK 36

If you grew up in church you've probably heard the phrase, "If it's God's will," followed by something along the lines of "He will heal me" or some other issue. God's Word is perfectly clear when it comes to salvation, healing, and many other issues. What the Bible is not crystal clear on is what you should do with your life. What does this mean? It means the will of God can be both present and continuous. The will of God is not a specific thing; however, it is every action and decision leading to a final destination.

Do not conform to the pattern of this
world, but be transformed by the
renewing of your mind. Then you

will be able to test and approve what God's will is—his good, pleasing and perfect will. -
Romans 12:2

Weekly Thought:

Have you ever wondered what it meant to be in God's will? Like Romans 12:2 says, don't behave like the rest of the world. We are going to mess up, we will slip, and we will fall. Get up when you do and keep moving.

Practical Application:

Let's ask God this week to reveal His will for our lives. He'll do so through the reading of His Word. Don't cheat yourself; give this one some thought. Really digest it.

Prayer

Heavenly Father, thank you for showing me your path, your will, and helping me to stay in your perfect and divine will. Amen.

SEPTEMBER

Give justice to the poor and the
orphan;
uphold the rights of the oppressed
and the destitute.
Rescue the poor and helpless;
deliver them from the grasp of evil
people.

— PSALM 82:3-4 NLT

BE ENCOURAGED

WEEK 37

Over time, if we do not take initiative to care for our bodies, our minds, and our spirits, we will begin to wear out. There are ways to avoid burn out, including taking breaks. It is important to give yourself time off away from work so you can recharge and be the best for your family and also your department. It is easy to allow the worries, stresses, and stuff you see day in and day out to bring you down over time. Give yourself rest, give yourself time away. Do not grow weary in well doing! Recharge, reload, and persist!

And as for you, brothers and sisters,
never tire of doing what is good.

— 2 THESSALONIANS 3:13

Weekly Thought:

It is easy for us to fall into the habit of taking on double shifts or working extra jobs to make ends meet. However, we have to remember to rest, to take breaks, and to get away to recharge our mind, body, and spirit.

Practical Application:

Ask God to recharge you this week. Take some time to enjoy a long weekend or plan one for the future. Take some time to enjoy your family, your spouse, your kids, or just alone.

Prayer

Heavenly Father, thank you for strength to endure difficult times, challenging circumstances, and power to conquer. Amen.

OUR HIGHER PROTECTION

WEEK 38

If you read some of the verses leading up to 2 Samuel 22:5, you will notice a very familiar passage of scripture. Interestingly, the praise David was writing in 2 Samuel 22 also found its way into Psalm 18, with a small variation. David had at some point been in a pretty nasty situation. In fact, he found himself in a lot of them! Imagine the worst situation you can be in: outnumbered, no radio communications, no backup, and weapon malfunction. God's got your back! Call on Him in troublesome times in life and He will deliver.

The waves of death swirled about me;
the torrents of destruction
overwhelmed me.

— 2 SAMUEL 22:5

Weekly Thought:

There are many stories, old and new, displaying the faithfulness of God to His people. Do you believe? Do you believe He provides us with supernatural protection? Think about this during the next week. What comes to mind when you recall God's protection over your life?

Practical Application:

Ask God to provide protection, deliverance, and restoration. Now, just believe!

Prayer

Heavenly Father, thank You for deliverance! Thank You for protection, even when I do not see the threat. -Amen

DRINK FROM THE WELL

WEEK 39

Listen, just because I am sitting here writing a devotional doesn't mean I believe the world is full of rainbows and unicorns. I know the reality of the world we live in and I know that strong men and women must stand ready to defend our communities, our states, and our country. This does not excuse us from being warriors washed in the Blood of Jesus, and renewed in His Word. It is time to make a change. Renew yourself by the reading of God's Word.

and have put on the new self, which
is being renewed in knowledge in
the image of its Creator.

— COLOSSIANS 3:10

Weekly Thought:

We can be men, women, law enforcement officers, SWAT team members, Negotiators, K9 Officers, or whatever specialty, armed with the supernatural power of God. Renew yourself through the reading of God's Word.

Practical Application:

This week, let the scripture prompt you to read more, pray more, and believe more. Ask God to give you a stronger appetite for His Word.

Prayer

Heavenly Father, Your love is my hiding place, and Your words renew my spirit. Thank you for the spiritual breath to fight. Amen

FAMILY OF ONE

WEEK 40

There are always going to be bad apples around us; not only in law enforcement, but in every profession and every entity. But, we know there is a special bond found in unity. What unifies us as law enforcement officers across borders, jurisdictions, and every division? Instead of finding reasons to complain this week let each of us look for reasons to celebrate and encourage each other. It is easy for us to begin to complain about something and fall down the slippery slope to constant negativity.

God sets the lonely in families,
he leads out the prisoners with
singing;

but the rebellious live in a sun-scorched land.

— PSALM 68:6

Weekly Thought:

There is something about the law enforcement profession that causes really nice people to become callused, cold, and hard-hearted. Take a step back this week and examine your heart.

Practical Application:

Ask God to soften your heart this week. He will give you the tools you need to begin moving forward in your walk with Him.

Prayer

Heavenly Father, restore families, and use me to bring peace and reconciliation. Amen.

OCTOBER

God is our refuge and strength,
always ready to help in times of trouble.
Psalm 46:1 NLT

DEALING WITH BETRAYAL

WEEK 41

Have you experienced the pain of betrayal? Someone you love as a brother or sister, and out of the blue, they betray your trust. Betrayal is something Jesus knew all too well. When Judas sold Jesus for silver (money), he played a key role in each of our salvation.

Jesus paid the ultimate price and was the perfect sacrifice for all of our mistakes. If you have experienced the pain and agony of betrayal, do not allow it to cause you to become bitter. Find some good out of this situation and be wise about your decisions.

At that time many will turn away
from the faith and will betray and
hate each other,

— MATTHEW 24:10

Weekly Thought:

At some time or another we will face betrayal. It likely won't be the same level of betrayal Jesus faced by Judas; however, each of us deal with this type of hurt in different ways. Allow God to use these situations to develop you and make you stronger and wiser.

Practical Application:

Ask God this week to show you how to navigate through tumultuous relationships. These are perilous times we live in and, unfortunately, it seems everyone is out for themselves. Do not allow the actions of others to determine your attitude, thereby affecting your destiny.

Prayer

Heavenly Father, I rest in the fact that You will

never leave me, that You will be by my side forever. Amen.

DULY APPOINTED

WEEK 42

We have been appointed to specific positions as law enforcement officers. There are days we may ask God, like Job does in chapter seven, "Why do we suffer? These are perilous times we live in and unfortunately, it seems everyone is out for themselves. However, as we lean on Him for wisdom, understanding, and divine leadership, we will find guidance and direction. Job endured tremendous turmoil in his life but he never cursed God.

While at times we want to ask God questions, we may never know the answers to certain things. We should also thank God for the opportunity to be responsible for such challenges. He has appointed us as leaders in troublesome times.

> *"Do not mortals have hard*
> *service on earth?*
> *Are not their days like those of*
> *hired laborers?*
>
> — JOB 7:1

Weekly Thought:

We have a tremendous responsibility every time we prepare for duty. We have a responsibility to ensure each of us as individuals returns home safely, and that each of our brothers and sisters return home safely as well. Let us take time to correct any flaws in our attitudes that may have developed over the years, including our outlook on life.

Practical Application:

If you need to, find a professional to talk to. For many law enforcement officers it is difficult to express issues by talking about them. Ask God this week to give you the courage to talk to someone who can help you. When you pray, consider praying for God to change your attitude, if it has become predominately negative.

Prayer

Heavenly Father, thank you for the call to serve your people as a law enforcement officer. Help me never to forget why I exist. Amen.

CONFIRMED & WANTED

WEEK 43

Each jurisdiction varies, but most require that an outstanding warrant be confirmed before a suspect is arrested and taken to jail. What has God confirmed in your life? The words Daniel spoke in chapter nine during his prayer to God have some similarities in meaning as it relates to confirmation.

For example, if God said, "There will be a great flood and it will destroy the entire earth," the confirmation of these words would be a terrible flood. God has spoken a word over your life and we know God does not intend or desire for any of us to be harmed or enslaved by bondage.

You have fulfilled the words spoken
against us and against our rulers
by bringing on us great disaster...

— DANIEL 9:12

Weekly Thought:

You may have heard words of negativity spoken over your life in the past. Maybe you've heard people you love tell you that you're not good enough. Maybe someone you loved and trusted told you that you will never make it in life and you will never change. Today, I am telling you differently. God created you in His image and He does not fail.

Practical Application:

Ask God to show you how He sees you. If you are a father and you have children, God may show you how He sees you through being a father. Either way, you were created to be blessed. Follow the principles of God's word, walk the walk of His word, and you will find the negative words of others to be unconfirmed.

Prayer

Heavenly Father, thank you that Your promises are always confirmed as "yes and amen" in my life. Amen.

YOU HAVE WHAT IT TAKES

WEEK 44

One evening, King Belshazzar had a real fancy banquet. In this banquet, those in attendance celebrated, ate food, and were having a merry good time. Daniel stepped up to the plate and began giving the "king" some words from God. The word *TEKEL*, as seen in Daniel 5:27, means "weighed". Essentially, King Belshazzar had been audited and did not have what it took to be king. Do not be the guy who can't cut it, or the veteran who thinks he knows everything, or even the new guy who comes up short when the game is on the line. Step up, follow the principles of God's Word, apply your knowledge and training, and celebrate your victory.

Tekel: You have been weighed on the scales and found wanting.

— DANIEL 5:27

Weekly Thought:

Do you know how it feels to be promoted or transferred to your dream job? Do you ever grow complacent? Do you settle in and believe you have arrived? Do not follow the example of failed leaders. Follow God and be a servant leader.

Practical Application:

Ask God to show you how and where your areas of improvement lie. Maybe these areas are not professionally related; maybe they are relational. Ask God. He will show you, and His Word will guide you.

Prayer

Heavenly Father, I know that because of Your word and Spirit I can do all things, because of Your Son, Jesus. Amen.

NOVEMBER

A final word: Be strong in the Lord and in his mighty power.

— EPHESIANS 6:10 NLT

BUT FIRST, SEEK WISDOM

WEEK 45

Be assured that I do not claim to be the smartest man alive. In fact, many of my colleagues would agree! However, if King Solomon, arguably the wisest man to ever live, advised us to seek wisdom above all things, I believe we should listen to his advice! It does not matter what profession you're in now or where you hope to go, the wisdom you seek will guide you like a light among the darkness.

The beginning of wisdom is this: Get
wisdom.
Though it cost all you have, get
understanding.

— PROVERBS 4:7

Weekly Thought:

I have mentioned wisdom a couple of different times over the past forty-four weeks. The reason is because it is paramount to our success. Please, seek wisdom.

Practical Application:

Simply put, ask God to give you wisdom. Maybe in your mind right now you are saying, "I need money to pay my bills! I can't make it on a policeman's salary!" Let me tell you, God will give you wisdom. As King Solomon said, seek wisdom above all things!

Prayer

Heavenly Father, before I ask for anything, remind me by Your Spirit to seek Your wisdom. Amen.

NEVER STOP LEARNING

WEEK 46

You may be wondering what the difference between the term *knowledge* and the term *wisdom* is. Knowledge is easiest defined as the obtaining of skills. Wisdom is having knowledge and experience. *Prudence* is having the foresight to look into the future. Do not settle for just the skills you currently have. Expand your portfolio! Expand your skillset! Explore training opportunities!

The heart of the discerning acquires
knowledge,
for the ears of the wise seek it out.

— PROVERBS 18:15

Weekly Thought:

Let's take a second to look at what Proverbs 18:15 is really saying: the heart of a man who thinks about the future seeks additional skills. If you desire a better future, build a variety of skills. Translation: never stop learning!

Practical Application:

Look for training opportunities in your current position. Consider going back to school, obtaining an advanced degree, or becoming an instructor in law enforcement. God's Word encourages us to never stop learning!

Prayer

Heavenly Father, teach me your ways and I will walk in them. Amen.

BE ON THE LOOKOUT

WEEK 47

Throughout the past forty-six weeks I have given you message after message of encouragement. I have shown you the love of a merciful God, and by now, I am sure He has shown His strengths to you and blessed you in many ways. Maybe you have been reading this in one sitting and not over eleven months or so. Maybe you once possessed a strong belief, but have fallen to the wayside.

Know this: God has a BOLO out for you. He longs for a relationship with you. God longs to have you in fellowship with Him and He longs to bless you. Consider the fact that the Sovereign God, the only one true God, is looking for you. He hasn't moved. Seek the face of God.

> *"Who dares despise the day of small things, since the seven eyes of the Lord that range throughout the earth will rejoice when they see the chosen capstone in the hand of Zerubbabel?"*
>
> – ZECHARIAH 4:10

Weekly Thought:

I am convinced that the greatest miracle ever is when a man, woman, boy, or girl, turn their lives over to Jesus. When someone like myself, who used to ingest large amounts of alcohol, partied all the time, smoked, cursed, and did many things against my convictions, is convicted by the Holy Spirit and is forgiven—that's a true miracle. God is waiting for you with open arms.

Practical Application:

You can stop what you are doing right now. There are no magical prayers. There are no magical words.

On the last page of this book is a prayer, just in case you need a prompt. Ask Jesus to forgive you. Thank Him for sacrificing His Son to pay for all of our sins. Welcome Him into your life, into your heart, and tell Him you believe. If you need someone to talk to, find a fellow law enforcement officer who follows Christ and ask that person to mentor you in the faith.

Prayer

Heavenly Father, may my eyes be always open and watching for You and aware of the threats of the enemy. Amen.

SPOTLIGHT ON CRIME

WEEK 48

Where has God brought you from? Are you better off today than you were in the past? Count your blessings! Consider the words of David in Psalm 107:14 when he praised God for bringing people from the darkness and bondage into a place of freedom. Today, as a peacemaker, you are set free! Not from being in custody or under arrest, but from your sins. Like I mentioned earlier, sin leads to guilt.

Guilt leads to other issues. God removes guilt with forgiveness of sin. Not only do these principles discussed throughout this devotional apply to all of us, but we can share them with others! Set someone free today with your words! There is great power in your words.

> *He brought them out of darkness, the*
> *utter darkness,*
> *and broke away their chains.*
>
> — PSALM 107:14

Weekly Thought:

You probably remember the first time you had to clear a building for whatever reason, (burglar alarm, burglary in progress, etc.). What a difference a good, quality light makes in a dark place! God is like this kind of light: so much more than good, so much He cannot be compared to others!

Practical Application:

Whenever you reach for your flashlight, think about the fact God has brought us from dark places into a life of freedom in Jesus! Begin your prayer today by just thanking Him for everything He has done in your life, and everything He will do!

Prayer

Heavenly Father, thank you for equipping me to serve as light in a dark world, because of Your Son Jesus. Amen.

DECEMBER

If the world hates you, remember that it hated me first.

— JOHN 15:18 NLT

WOUNDED SPIRITS

WEEK 49

What wounds us physically may not wound us mentally, emotionally, or spiritually. However, what wounds us spiritually wounds the rest of our bodies and every part of our being. If you are wounded, and I mean the type of wound that is so deep under the surface, it may be time to take action against it and pursue real healing.

Maybe your wounds are hidden, ones that come from previous incidents while on duty. Or maybe they are from previous relationships, or from your father or mother. It is time to address the wounded spirits of men and women, especially those who are with us in law enforcement.

The spirit of a man will sustain his infirmity; but a wounded spirit who can bear?

— PROVERBS 18:14

Weekly Thought:

Again, you may consider seeking advice from a pastor, chaplain, or someone you trust and believe in to talk with. God is more than able to heal your wounds, no matter how you received them and how deeply they run.

Practical Application:

I believe men and women serving in law enforcement need to address their issues caused by previous incidents on the job (officer involved shootings, violent encounters, etc.). God has paid the price for your healing. Ask Him today in your time of prayer to begin a work to heal those deep wounds in your spirit. Do. Not. Quit.

Prayer

Heavenly Father, thank you for soothing and healing

my wounds, and for using me to ease the pain other's experience. Amen.

KEY TO VICTORY-MENTAL TOUGHNESS

WEEK 50

Everyone has different strengths. You may be super strong when it comes to lifting weights while the next guy may be super strong when it comes to running marathons. We are a team, however. Not everyone will have the same strengths. An area of law enforcement that needs additional attention and training is mental toughness.

Not that law enforcement officers are not mentally tough, but how many struggle with mental issues after a traumatic incident? It's time to take our thoughts into captivity and command them to submit to the Word of God, and we can do this with the power of the Spirit of God. Healing is a command away.

> *I can do all this through him who gives me strength.*
>
> — PHILIPPIANS 4:13

Weekly Thought:

If you have thoughts of hurting yourself or taking your own life, please talk to someone immediately. There is hope for you. There is a future for you. Your life is not defined by your past mistakes and you are uniquely made by God for a purpose. God has a plan for you and for your life. Find someone to talk to. Get some help. People care about you and whatever trouble you are facing, it is not the end.

Practical Application:

I thought at one time I was the only one who had horrible thoughts, dreams, and experiences. After seeing some of the things we see on a regular basis I've learned these things are expected. The line is drawn when you consider hurting yourself or someone else. In the name of Jesus, I speak hope, healing, a future, and a purpose into your life.

YOU HAVE HOPE. His name is Jesus.

Prayer

Heavenly Father, when my mind roams, and my thoughts create anxiety, remind me to call them into order under the authority of your word. Amen.

YOU BECOME WHO YOU ASSOCIATE WITH

WEEK 51

Sometimes working in an adults-only environment can look a lot of being in high school. Just because you are invited or encouraged to do something questionable does not mean you have to, and just because it may not be wrong does not mean it is good for you.

Think about your circumstances, where you have come from, and where you want to be. Now, think about who to keep company with and use great wisdom and discernment as you make those choices.

Walk with the wise and become wise,
for a companion of fools suffers
harm.

— PROVERBS 13:20

Weekly Thoughts:

I have been there. I never consumed as much alcohol as when I entered the law enforcement profession. I realized that behavior was not fruitful to my life and I changed my ways. Excessive drinking wasn't wise and it wasn't going to get me to the place God has for me.

Practical Application:

Peer pressure can produce good results or it can produce very destructive results. I am not telling you what to do, but I am telling you to listen to the voice inside of you. Follow your convictions and ask yourself if your actions are wrong, or if they're just not producing fruit in your life.

Prayer

Heavenly Father, give me the common sense and discernment to know when I need to remove myself from other people. -Amen.

TIME TO ADVANCE

WEEK 52

Is it adrenaline that propels you through high stress situations or is it the power of God? Recall what God did for Daniel in the den of lions, or for David against a bear, or the outnumbered people of God in the stories we read in the Bible. What about David versus Goliath?

Do not be afraid. Darkness will not go away simply because you and I do not act. We cannot pretend evil does not exist. With God's power, with His help, we can do great things.

With your help I can advance against
a troop;
with my God I can scale a wall.

— PSALM 18:29

Weekly Thoughts:

This is the last weekly devotion of the book. I am here to tell you it's time to advance on the enemy. It is time for you to grow in Christ. By the power of God you will continue to heal, your lives will continue to be restored, and your faith will continually increase in Christ alone. God will use you to do great things!

Practical Application:

I pray this week that God seals up the work He is doing in your life. I pray God continues to increase you, to secure you in finances, and establish a buffer crop in your life. I pray this week that you continue to seek the face of Jesus, even beyond this book of devotions.

Prayer

Heavenly Father, thank you for the courage and boldness to pursue evil men and women. Guide my steps, Lord, so that I may honor You. Amen.

AFTERWORD

There are no magic words and no magic prayers, but below is a prayer you can pray if you do not know what to say. If you do not know Jesus, if you have never asked Him to come into your heart and into your life, now is the time. Do not delay.

Thank you for taking time to read *Spirit and Truth.* I invite you to contact me with any questions you may have. If God has used this writing to impact you, I would love to hear about it! God bless you, and remember—He's got your back!

In His Service

Adam Davis

PRAYER OF SALVATION

Heavenly Father,

I come to you thankful. I come to you thankful for the sacrifice you gave through your Son Jesus for me. You cared enough about me to give your very best. I am asking you to forgive me of all of my sins, all of my wrongdoings; wash me with the blood of the perfect sacrifice of Your Son, Jesus. I want you to come into my heart, into my life, and take over. I am asking you to take me into custody and lead my path. I am surrendering my life to you, Father God. Thank you for eternal life through your precious, sinless Son, Jesus! I believe in you; I believe Jesus died on a cross, rose from the grave, and reigns today with You!

Amen

If you prayed this prayer for the first time, or prayed this prayer at all, I would love to hear from you! Visit www.TheAdamDavis.com for more information.

ABOUT THE AUTHOR

Adam Davis has served in many law enforcement roles throughout his career. He and his wife have been married for about fifteen years and have three children. Davis will graduate in December 2015 with a degree in political science and public administration.

For More Information

www.TheAdamDavis.com

CPSIA information can be obtained
at www.ICGtesting.com
Printed in the USA
BVHW041445120120
569205BV00005B/103/P